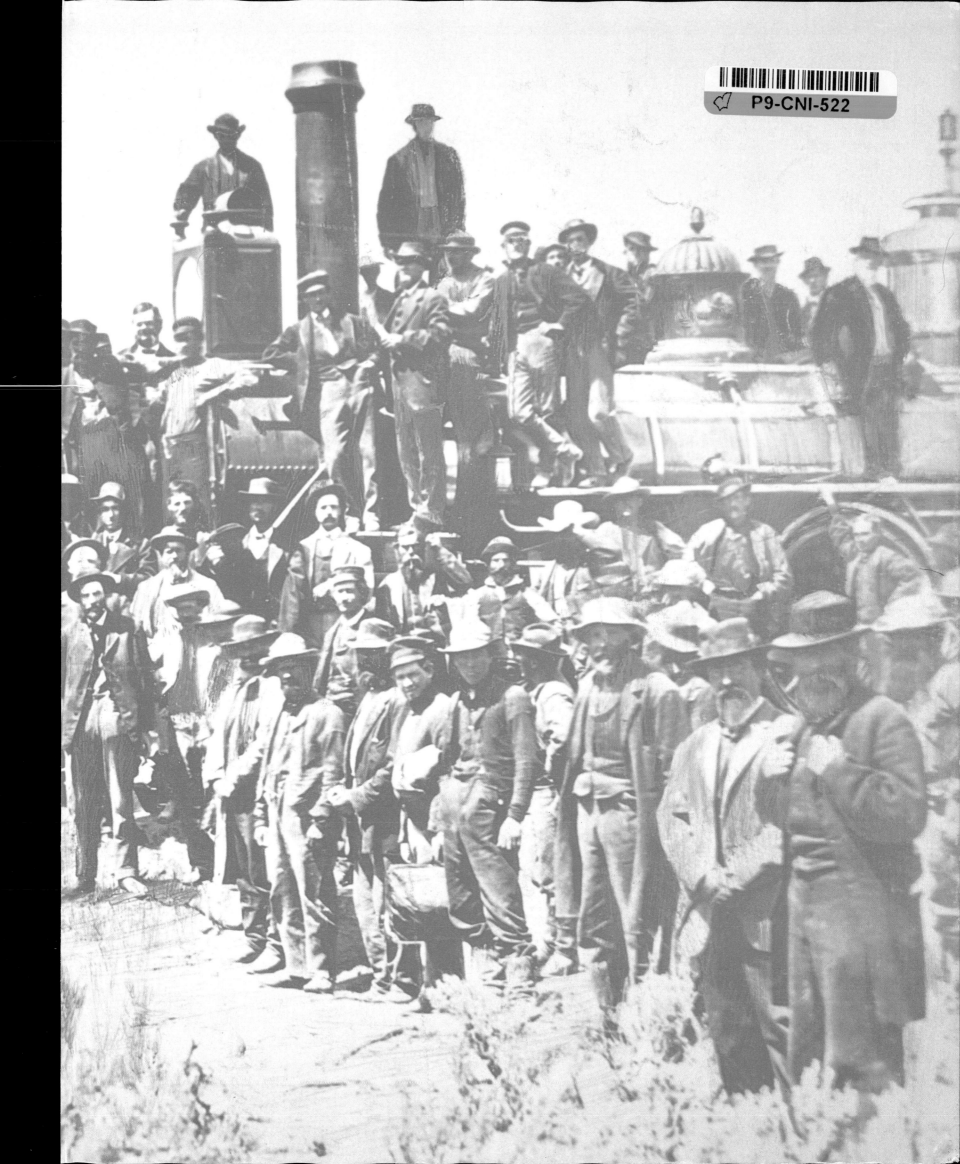

THE WILD WEST

Mike Stotter

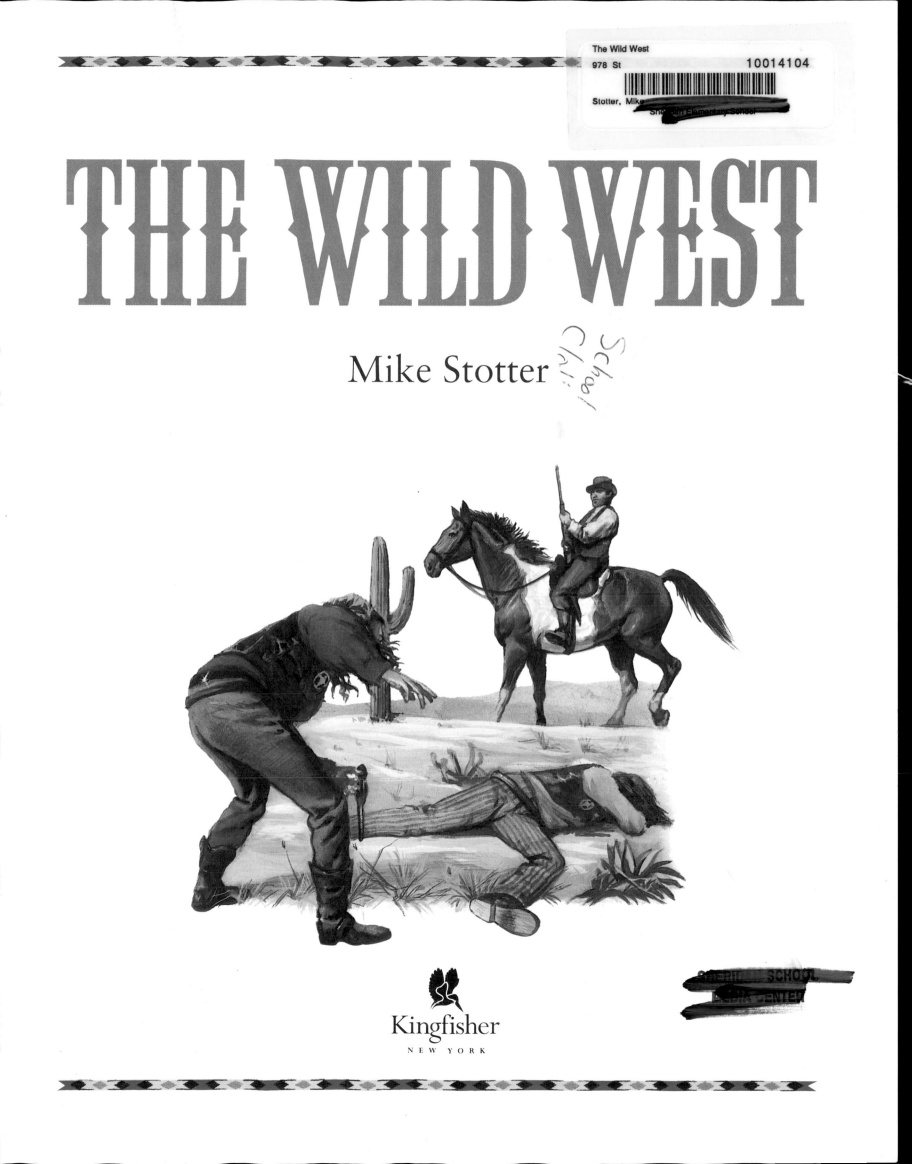

Kingfisher

NEW YORK

KINGFISHER
Larousse Kingfisher Chambers Inc.
95 Madison Avenue
New York, New York 10016

First edition 1997
10 9 8 7 6 5 4 3 2 1

Copyright © Larousse plc 1997

LIBRARY OF CONGRESS CATALOGING-IN-PUBLICATION DATA
Stotter, Mike.
    The wild West / Mike Stotter; consultant, Dee Brown.—1st
American ed.
        p.   cm.
    Includes index.
    1. Frontier and pioneer life—West (U.S.)—Juvenile literature.
2. West (U.S.)—History—Juvenile literature.   I. Title.
F596.S9   1997
978—dc21 96-52789 CIP AC

ISBN 0-7534-5085-2

Consultant: Dee Brown
Editor: Clare Oliver
Design: Ben White Associates and Terry Woodley
Cover design: Terry Woodley
Cover illustration: Kenny McKendry, Artist Partners
Art editor: Christina Fraser
Picture research: Veneta Bullen
Printed in Italy

THE AUTHOR

Mike Stotter has long been fascinated by the Wild West.
To date, his books have been mostly fictional—he has
written six pulp Western novels. He has also contributed
to *Twentieth Century Western Writers* and the
Encyclopedia of Frontier and Western Fiction. He and his
family have settled some way east of the frontier, in
Essex, England.

THE CONSULTANT

Dee Brown is a leading expert on the American West. He
is most renowned for *Bury My Heart at Wounded Knee*,
which has sold more than five million copies worldwide.
He has written more than 20 works of fiction and
nonfiction relating to American frontier history. He lives
with his wife in Little Rock, Arkansas.

CONTENTS

EARLY DAYS

Native Americans had lived undisturbed throughout North and South America until the European discovery of the "New World" in 1492. Now the countries of Europe raced to claim the rich "new" land for themselves. But it was the Spanish conquistadors who had the greatest impact on the native people.

To the southwest came Francisco Vásquez de Coronado and to the east Hernando de Soto. Both men had orders from the king of Spain to find the legendary "Seven Cities of Gold." Despite vast armies of men and animals, neither man found the mythical treasure.

The Spanish treated the Pueblo Indians of New Mexico very harshly. In 1680 they fought back, killing almost 400 Spaniards and stealing their horses. Until then, dogs had carried heavy loads, but now the horse, called "big dog," took its place. Within 100 years, most tribes used horses. On horseback, Native Americans could hunt farther afield.

What the Spaniards couldn't gain by trade, they took by force. Hostile villages were attacked and plundered. The defenders' arrows, lances, and war clubs were no match for the invaders' rifles and steel swords. The conquistadors enslaved the men and boys and took the women as cooks and servants.

▼ In 1783, colonists in the east declared their independence from Britain, and the United States was born. Until the early 1800s, vast areas of the continent remained colonies belonging to Spain, France, and Britain.

But gradually the United States started to expand its boundaries. Sometimes it fought for territory, as it did with Britain in 1812. It also bought land. In 1803, Napoleon sold the Louisiana Territory to the United States for $15 million.

BRITISH (until 1818)

FRENCH (The Louisiana Purchase, 1803)

SPANISH (Mexican after 1823)

THE UNITED STATES 1783

N

MILES 500
KM 800

KEY TO STATES WITH DATES THEY JOINED THE UNION
1 Michigan 1837
2 Illinois 1818
3 Indiana 1816
4 Ohio 1803
5 Vermont 1791
6 Maine 1820
7 Missouri 1821
8 Kentucky 1792
9 Arkansas 1836
10 Tennessee 1796
11 Louisiana 1812
12 Mississippi 1817
13 Alabama 1819
14 Florida 1819

The wild frontier

In 1803, President Jefferson bought the Louisiana Territory from the French. The land stretched all the way from the Mississippi River to the eastern slopes of the Rocky Mountains. Expeditions set out to map the West. Many of the early explorers, such as Zebulon Pike, Jim Bridger, and Thomas "Brokenhand" Fitzpatrick, became the first settlers of the wild frontier, trapping furs in the mountains for their living. The West captured the imagination as a place of opportunity, freedom, and rich land. The rush to settle the West had begun.

Early explorers

Meriwether Lewis and William Clark captained the "Corps of Discovery," an expedition to explore the Louisiana Territory and reach the Pacific coast. They took three boats, laden with gifts and trading goods, and 30 men. Clark brought along his black slave, York. They also hired a young Shoshoni girl, named Sacajawea, to be their guide and interpreter. The expedition took over a year to cross the Rockies along the Oregon Trail, and reached the coast in 1805.

Mountain man of legend

James "Tomahawk" Beckwourth headed west from Virginia in 1826. There he met a Crow Indian woman who claimed he was her long lost son, and she named him Morning Star. The tribe adopted him, and he fought alongside Crow warriors against the Blackfeet. He became a war chief, and he was even married to a chief's two daughters at the same time. He later worked as a government guide and interpreter. He found a route through the Sierra Nevada Mountains to California, and it was named the Beckwourth Pass after him.

▶ *Fall of the Alamo*, by Robert Onderdonk

▲ In the early 1830s, Texas was under Mexican control. A small Spanish mission and fortress called the Alamo was the site of a bloody 12-day siege in 1836. All 182 Texan defenders, including the famous Davy Crockett, Jim Bowie, and Colonel William Travis, were massacred by 3,000 Mexican troops. But six weeks later Texas finally won its independence with the stirring battle cry, "Remember the Alamo!" In 1845, Texas joined the Union and became the 28th state. This new land continued the westward expansion of American control. And thanks to the large herds of cattle there, Texas was settled by ranchers and cowboys, and became a vital part of the West's cattle industry.

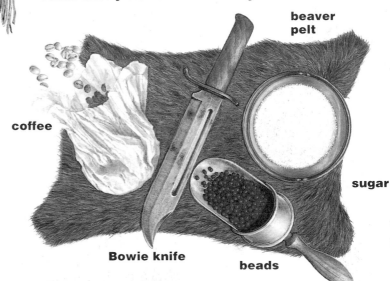

coffee • Bowie knife • beads • beaver pelt • sugar

Trading at Rendezvous

After lonely trapping in the wilds, the highlight of a mountain man's year was the month-long meeting called Rendezvous. He traded his furs for knives, sugar, and gunpowder. But best of all, there was plenty of whiskey, gambling, and horse-racing!

Clues to the past

The true days of the Wild West ended over a hundred years ago, but we can still find out about that time. Paintings, photographs, diaries, letters, newspapers, and various other Native American artifacts allow historians to build up a picture of how the people of the West lived—and died—in those days.

► *The Cowboy*, by Frederic Remington

◄ If you couldn't write down words, how would you keep a record of your family history or honor a dead chief? Totem poles are found mainly in the far northwest of the United States. Some tell of a tribe's ancestors; "shame poles" were built to disgrace people; others were upright coffins, containing a dead body. Like this Kwakiutl totem pole, many still stand today, and they tell us a lot about the way of life of the Native Americans who carved and painted them.

Native American artifacts

1 Ice Age stone weapon point, found at Folsom, New Mexico
2 Chipewyan caribou bone scraper
3 Papago pot
4 Ute moccasins
5 Potawatomi pipe
6 Pima coiled basket
7 Naiche painting on doeskin
8 Navajo blanket
9 Iroquois carved antler comb

Photography

The first photograph was taken in 1826, and the time of the Wild West is one of the earliest in history to be recorded by photos. Pictures have survived of everything from the unspoiled landscapes to the characters who lived there—cowboys, settlers, goldminers, and Native Americans.

On canvas

Painters George Catlin, Karl Bodmer, Mary Foote, and Albert Bierstadt knew that they had to capture the Wild West before it vanished forever. Frederic Remington and Charles Russell rode alongside cowboys and soldiers, recording what they saw in beautiful paintings.

The written word

Ordinary diaries, like that of Susan Shelby Magoffin, were simple accounts of everyday experiences. Many early settlers wrote private diaries that were later published. Accounts of frontier life by famous explorers sold in huge numbers at the time, to readers eager for excitement. Guidebooks are also a valuable source of firsthand information; they were written to let a settler know what to expect and to describe the conditions on a wagon train.

▼ Using wool from their own sheep, Navajo women wove these splendid, colorful blankets so tight that they were almost waterproof. Even the smallest took weeks to complete.

Susan Shelby Magoffin

In a typical Dakota (Sioux) village on the Plains, a stream provided water, cottonwood trees supplied firewood, young spring grass fed the horses, and there was plenty of open space to pitch the tepees.

It took up to 12 buffalo hides to make a family tepee. It was the women who made, owned, and erected the tepees, stretching the hides over pine poles. A fire inside kept everyone warm in winter, while in summer the sides were lifted to let the breeze in.

Games were enjoyed by old and young alike. Men and boys played stickball, which was known as "little brother of war" because many ended up with cuts or even broken bones! Horse races were popular, too, and men liked to gamble with stones and straws.

▶ Only the women made robes. The buffalo skin was pegged out, scraped of all flesh, then washed with water and grease. Once cleaned, the skin was left to dry in the sun. Then the women rubbed it for days until it was soft and pliable.

TEPEE LIFE

Each Native American tribe had its own way of life, suited to its surroundings. But all tribes had a similar social structure. The three most important men were the chief, the medicine man, and the war chief. Next came the elders and warriors, then the squaws and children. Like other Plains Indians, the Dakota (Sioux) lived in villages. Life was hard. Those children who survived were cared for by all the members of the tribe. They had toys, games, and pet puppies. Boys practiced with bows and arrows. Dolls were popular with the girls, who learned the skills they needed for adult life from their mothers.

▲ To make pemmican, cut buffalo meat into narrow strips and dry slowly over a fire or in the sun. Pound this "jerky" and mix with chokecherries and buffalo fat. In sacks, it can last for five years.

▶ After the chief, the most important man was the medicine man, or shaman. He was the contact between the real world and the spirit world. He cured illnesses with his magic and medicine.

11

Tribal homelands

Native Americans often moved with the seasons. Some tribes, such as the Arapaho, followed the migrating buffalo. They spent the hot summer months in the cool north and moved south as it grew colder. With the coming of the horse, it was much easier for people to move around freely.

Almost half of the North American Indian tribes were based between the Mississippi River and the Rocky Mountains. But tribes were often forced out of their original homelands either by white settlers or by other jealous tribes. The eastern tribes were the first to obtain guns, and used them to push other tribes west and steal their land.

Who lived where?

The map shows the homelands of the different Native American tribes. Though each tribe was distinct and usually had its own language, tribes are sometimes grouped together by area. The four western areas are the Southwest, Plains, Northwest Coast, and California-Intermountain. The other, non-Western areas are the Far North, Caribbean, Middle American, and Eastern Woodlands.

Western tribes

Frontiersmen and settlers encountered many, many tribes in the Wild West. The social structure of a tribe was based on family groups. Many tribes named themselves after their holy ancestors. These spiritual guardians were known as the "totem" and often took the form of an animal.

Tlingit
Northwest Coast

Hupa
California-Intermountain

Pawnee
Plains

Types of dwelling

Depending on what building material was to hand, different tribes had different types of houses. Pueblos (1) were built from adobe bricks, tepees (2) from hides, wigwams (3) of bark and leaves, and lodges (4) from earth and wood.

Navajo
Southwest

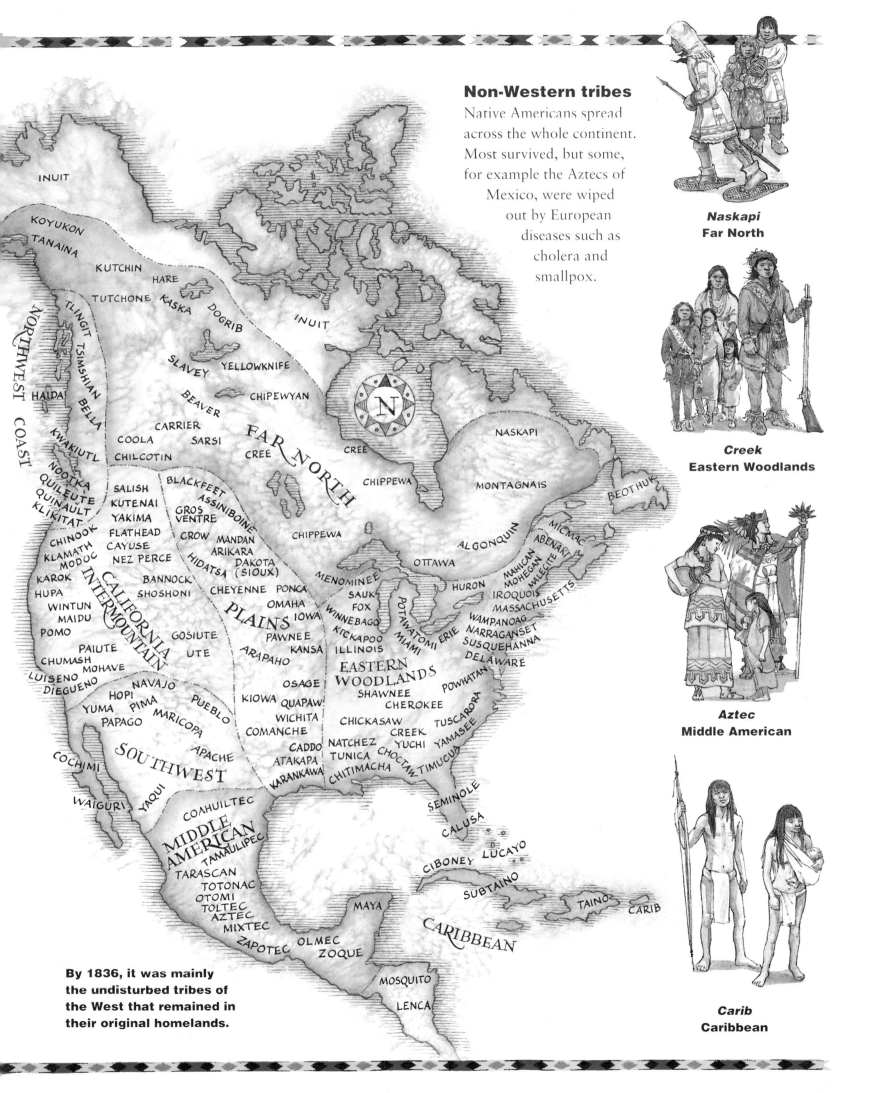

Non-Western tribes

Native Americans spread across the whole continent. Most survived, but some, for example the Aztecs of Mexico, were wiped out by European diseases such as cholera and smallpox.

Naskapi
Far North

Creek
Eastern Woodlands

Aztec
Middle American

Carib
Caribbean

INUIT

KOYUKON
TANAINA
KUTCHIN
HARE
TUTCHONE KASKA
DOGRIB
INUIT
SLAVEY
YELLOWKNIFE
BEAVER
CHIPEWYAN
NORTHWEST COAST
TLINGIT
TSIMSHIAN
HAIDA
BELLA
KWAKIUTL
NOOTKA
QUILEUTE
QUINAULT
KLIKITAT
CARRIER
COOLA
SARSI
CHILCOTIN
FAR NORTH
CREE
CREE
NASKAPI
CHIPPEWA
MONTAGNAIS
BEOTHUK

SALISH
KUTENAI
YAKIMA
FLATHEAD
CAYUSE
NEZ PERCE
BLACKFEET
ASSINIBOINE
GROS VENTRE
CROW
MANDAN
ARIKARA
DAKOTA (SIOUX)
HIDATSA
CHIPPEWA
ALGONQUIN
MICMAC
ABENAKI
MAHICAN
MOHEGAN
MALECITE
CHINOOK
KLAMATH
MODOC
KAROK
HUPA
WINTUN
MAIDU
POMO
BANNOCK
SHOSHONI
CALIFORNIA INTERMOUNTAIN
GOSIUTE
UTE
PAIUTE
CHUMASH
MOHAVE
LUISENO
DIEGUENO
CHEYENNE
PLAINS
PONCA
OMAHA
IOWA
PAWNEE
ARAPAHO
KANSA
OTTAWA
MENOMINEE
SAUK
FOX
WINNEBAGO
KICKAPOO
POTAWATOMI
MIAMI
ILLINOIS
HURON
ERIE
IROQUOIS
MASSACHUSETTS
WAMPANOAG
NARRAGANSET
SUSQUEHANNA
DELAWARE

HOPI
YUMA
PIMA
PAPAGO
MARICOPA
NAVAJO
PUEBLO
OSAGE
KIOWA
QUAPAW
WICHITA
COMANCHE
CADDO
ATAKAPA
KARANKAWA
EASTERN WOODLANDS
SHAWNEE
CHEROKEE
POWHATAN
CHICKASAW
CREEK
TUSCARORA
NATCHEZ
TUNICA
YUCHI
CHOCTAW
YAMASEE
TIMUCUA
CHITIMACHA
APACHE
SOUTHWEST

COCHIMI
WAIGURI
YAQUI
COAHUILTEC
MIDDLE AMERICAN
TAMAULIPEC
TARASCAN
TOTONAC
OTOMI
TOLTEC
AZTEC
MIXTEC
ZAPOTEC
OLMEC
ZOQUE
MAYA
SEMINOLE
CALUSA
CIBONEY
LUCAYO
SUBTAINO
TAINO
CARIB
CARIBBEAN

MOSQUITO
LENCA

By 1836, it was mainly the undisturbed tribes of the West that remained in their original homelands.

13

Hunting and food

Some tribes were hunters, relying on buffalo and other game for food, shelter, and clothing. Most Native Americans gathered foods from the wild, too. Tribes such as the Mandans, who lived in areas of good soil, were excellent farmers. In fact, 60 percent of the crops we grow today come from plants first cultivated by Native Americans. They include corn, beans, tomatoes, squash, potatoes, chili peppers, vanilla, tobacco, and cotton. There were also medicinal herbs, host plants that gave wax, and plants for vegetable dyes.

Using the buffalo

Every part of the buffalo was used. The meat fed the family, while soap made from the fat kept them clean. Bones were carved into tools and knives, and the hide made clothing, tepees, and shields. The thick hair was woven into rope or used for children's toys.

BUFFALO BY-PRODUCTS
1 sacred decorated skull
2 toy made of buffalo hair
3 leather war shield
4 pemmican hammer of leather and bone
5 buffalo-skin blanket

The buffalo runners

Before the days of rifles, hunting buffalo was a dangerous business. A hunter would ride in close, select one buffalo, and herd it away from the others. A skilled hunter could kill a small herd in about 15 minutes, but if he wasn't careful, he could be thrown from his horse and be stampeded to death by the panicking animals.

Tasty harvest

Corn (1), beans, and squash (2) were the three main crops and were often called the Trinity. Women grew them in their own gardens. Sunflowers (3) were grown for their nutritious seeds, and rice (4) was gathered from the wild. Vanilla pods and wild berries (5) were used in cooking and preserving.

Preparing the corn

Corn was part of the Native American's staple diet. Women ground the kernels into flour between two stones. To make corn fritters, they added water to the flour, then fried the cakes in a skillet over the fire.

15

The wolf headdress shows this warrior is a scout.

What's your name?

Some children were not named until they were teenagers. Like many, the Apache chief Black Eagle got his name through a vision (1). He earned his name by taking part in a horse-stealing raid, where he saw the eagle from his dream (2). Black Eagle went on to become chief of his tribe (3).

1

Warriors

Not only did tribes fight the white settlers and the soldiers, they warred among themselves to gain new territory and to prove their courage. The Dakota (Sioux) were great enemies of the Crow and Pawnees. The Comanche were swift and ferocious on horseback, and everyone feared the Apaches. Eagle-feather bonnets, known as "war bonnets," were worn only by those who earned them by their acts of bravery. Others wore simple headbands or skullcaps.

coup stick

A horse's warpaint showed how many raids it had made.

Cheyenne warrior

◄ Warriors would kill and even scalp the enemy, but one of the most repected war deeds was "counting coup"—touching the enemy but not killing him. The more coups counted, the greater a man's status as a warrior. Many used a special, curved stick, called a coup stick, which they decorated with eagle feathers. The feathers showed previous war honors.

Dressed to kill

In addition to their headdresses, which showed their position within their tribe's warrior society, warriors donned warpaint for spiritual protection. Comanches used black and white; Crows had red-striped faces for horse-stealing raids; and the Blackfeet painted a white line across the face for vengeance.

Comanche

Crow

Blackfoot

Weapons of war

An elk-horn bow could fire fatal arrows over a short range, but for closer combat a warrior favored an iron-headed tomahawk or stone-headed war club. Lances were thrust forward to gut or dismount an enemy rider, so most carried a shield for protection.

war lance

shield

tomahawk

war club

quiver holding bow and arrows

The warrior society was a kind of club for selected men of the tribe. In battle the warriors followed the war chief, a man picked for his leadership and fighting skills. In peacetime the society acted as the tribe's police force. Members were known for their discipline and fierceness. Loyalty to their tribe and society was to the death.

The sun dance ceremony

A warrior reaffirmed his pledge to his tribe by taking part in a religious ceremony called the sun dance. For eight days he had no food or drink and gazed into the sun wearing body paint. His chest was pierced with skewers, tied by long leather thongs to a sacred pole. He danced and jerked until the flesh gave way, leaving scars which he wore with pride.

Religion and myth

To every Native American, the Earth and the spirit life were the most important matters in the world. All tribes believed in a spiritual force that was in the Earth, animals, the sky, and everything around them. They paid their respect in rituals and ceremonies, some adapting elements from the Christianity imported by the Spanish.

A young girl's vigil

Every young teenager performed a vigil as part of the journey into adulthood. Catherine Wabose became her tribe's prophetess after hers. Following a six-day fast, she heard a supernatural voice tell her to walk along a shining path. First she met "Everlasting Standing Woman," then "Little Man Spirit," who said his name would be her first son's name. "Bright Blue Sky" gave her the gift of life. Finally she received the gift of prophecy.

Sweat it out

Though it varied from tribe to tribe, the sweat lodge ceremony was universal among the American Indians. It was used to purify the soul or heal sickness. The sweat lodge was dome-shaped, built with saplings, and covered with blankets or hide. It seated about six people. A leader in charge of the ceremony threw herbs and water over the heated stones in the firepit, which gave off purifying steam. The participants sat in the lodge chanting and praying to the spirits.

Many dances, prayers, and ceremonies were performed for special occasions. Even at its end, a Native American's life was spent trying to please the spirits. Tribes such as the Dakota built tall platforms on which they placed their dead, to bring them closer to the sky. So that their history was remembered, mythical stories like that of the Buffalo Dance were handed down by word of mouth from generation to generation.

The ghost dance

The ghost dance was practiced by tribes of the Plains and Great Basin. A Paiute prophet named Wovoka told his ghost dancers that praying, chanting, and dancing in circles for days would bring back dead relatives and the buffalo, and even return the land to the way it had been before the white man came. The ghost dancers wore shirts covered in symbols that were said to protect them from harm.

RANCHES AND RANCHERS

After the Civil War ended in 1865, Texas became the center of the cattle industry. Cowboys got their start in this western state where a cow cost $4 or $5, but might sell to beef-hungry easterners for $50.

Springtime roundup

In spring the cattle were driven down from their winter pasture into corrals. Riders would rope a calf and drag it to the branding crew. The red-hot iron marked a new calf with its owner's brand for life.

Line riders

The first ranches had no fences. Their boundaries were natural barriers, such as rivers. Line riders worked the remotest parts of the ranch making sure the cattle stayed on their side of the range, or line.

Food for all

Out in the middle of nowhere, a ranch had to be self-sufficient. Milk came from the dairy cows, eggs from the hen-house, and water from a stream or well. Meat was plentiful and a small kitchen garden supplied fresh vegetables.

Who's in charge?

When a ranch owner was away on business, the foreman was in charge. He hired and fired everyone from the cook to the cowboys, wranglers, and broncobusters.

There was plenty of free grassland and good water in the West—important ingredients for fattening cows. From Arizona to Colorado, Montana to Wyoming, cattle prices soared. "Cattle barons"

Charles Goodnight

grew rich on the success of the trade. Charles Goodnight was one of the best-known barons, and he's also famous for inventing

Elizabeth Iliff

the chuck wagon so that his cowboys ate well on the trail. John and Elizabeth Iliff supplied beef to the Union Pacific Railroad, buying up to 15,000 steers each year.

Richard King's running W

Mifflin Kenedy's laurel leaf

rocking chair

Brands

The best way to know who owned a cow was to read its brand. It was finders keepers if you found an orphaned calf with no brand (known as a maverick). Anyone could claim the unmarked calf and brand it as his own.

hog eye

broken arrow

scissors

pipe

21

A cowboy and his horse

The original cowboy was the Native American, taught to look after cattle by Spanish missionaries in Mexico. Mexican *vaqueros* came next. Theirs is the language of the cowboy: *lazo* became lasso, *reata* lariat, and *chaperjos* chaps. Known all over as the cowboy, he might also be called "cowpuncher," "cowhand," or "buckaroo," depending on which part of the country he worked in.

cowgirl
Montana

vaquero
Mexico, S. California, Arizona

buckaroo
California, Nevada, Oregon

cowpuncher
New Mexico, Texas

Rough 'n' tough

Honest, loyal, and hardworking, the cowboy always treated strangers with friendship. The land was harsh, and many suffered from rheumatism, eye diseases, and damaged spines. Most walked bowlegged from too many years in the saddle!

hat

quarter horse

bridle

bandanna

gloves

revolver

slicker

brand

blanket

chaps

spurs

stirrup

bit

reins

saddle

lariat

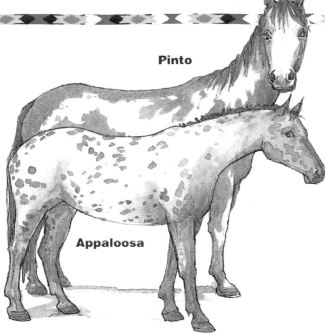

Pinto

Appaloosa

A cowboy chose a horse suited to the job and found a gelding more reliable than a mare. The strong, agile quarter horse was the most popular breed with cowboys. But some selected a horse for its looks, such as the Appaloosa, favorite of the Nez Percé Indians, or the dappled Pinto.

Spurs and saddles

Often called "gentle persuaders," spurs are used to control a horse. Sharp new spurs had the points blunted. There were two main styles of saddle, the Texas (1) and the California (2). A saddle lasted a lifetime, and there was an old cowboy saying, "to sell your saddle," which meant you were broke.

fancy spurs

workaday spurs

Cowboy gear

The cowboy's leather boots were handmade. Two-inch heels prevented the foot from slipping out of the stirrup. The cowboy's hat, often a Stetson, had a broad brim to protect the eyes from the sun and a tall crown to keep the head cool. Chaps, made either of leather or wool, were worn over jeans to protect the legs from thorns or prickly cacti. Having water could mean life or death, so the cowboy kept his canteen full and close at hand. A sougan, or quilted blanket, kept him warm at night. The cowboy's rifle was used for hunting and protection. It was carried in the chuck wagon along with his bed roll so it didn't get in his way.

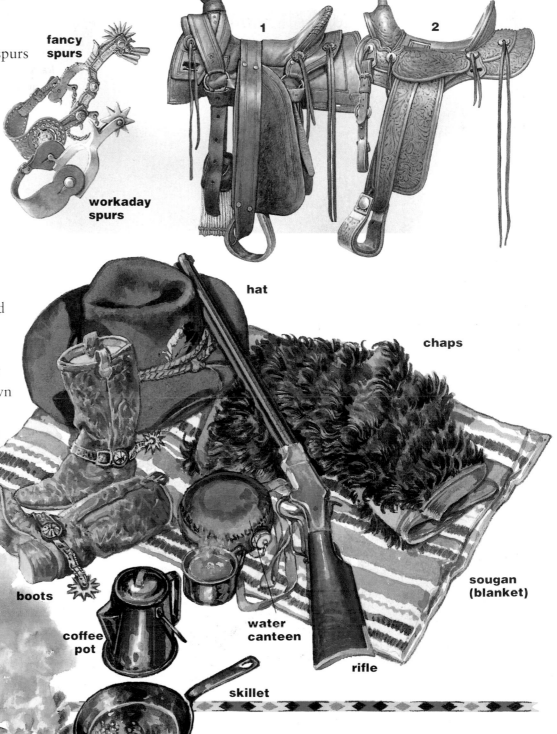

hat

chaps

boots

coffee pot

water canteen

sougan (blanket)

rifle

skillet

On the trail

On a cattle drive, there was one cowboy to every 250 cattle. A 1,200-mile drive took about four months, and the average cowboy earned $30 per month. The trail boss headed the column, which could be as wide as two miles. At the sides, flank riders stopped the steers from wandering away, while at the back the drag rider pushed them forward.

Life on the trail

Awake before dawn, a cowboy spent up to 14 hours in the saddle every day. The men took turns keeping watch at night.

Danger!

River crossings were dangerous, as many of the cowboys couldn't swim. It didn't take much to stampede nervous longhorns. Thunderstorms, grass fires, even a cowboy sneezing could set them running!

flank riders

chuck wagon

trail boss

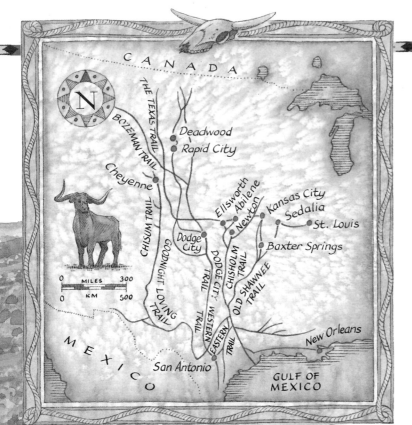

Cattle trail blazers

The cattle routes had to be carved out of harsh terrain. Rancher Charles Goodnight and his partner Oliver Loving founded the Goodnight-Loving Trail; Joseph McCoy's route used part of the Chisholm Trail; Granville Stuart drove his steers across Oregon to Montana, and Lucien Maxwell cut a new route to Nebraska called the Western Trail.

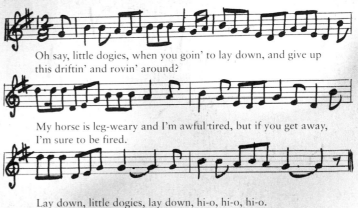

humped Brahman

Texas longhorn

Hereford

British shorthorn

drag riders

Breeds of cow

"Critters," "beeves," and "dogies" were the cowboys' favorite nicknames for cattle. The Texas longhorn was the predominant cow in the Southwest. Later, the shorthorn, the Hereford, and the humped Brahman were introduced. They provided better meat and were immune to "Texas tick."

Campfire songs

A sweet-singing cowboy entertained the men and calmed the cows. There were rousing trail-driving songs, like "The Old Chisholm Trail," as well as gentle lullabies.

The Night Herding Song

Oh say, little dogies, when you goin' to lay down, and give up this driftin' and rovin' around?

My horse is leg-weary and I'm awful tired, but if you get away, I'm sure to be fired.

Lay down, little dogies, lay down, hi-o, hi-o, hi-o.

▲ The chuck wagon and cook were a focal point on the drive. Bacon, bread, and beans were usually on the menu, while dried and canned food helped make meals varied. Strong black coffee was a must with every meal.

Cow towns

After long months on the trail, the cowboy hit town. He took a quick bath and shaved, threw away his old, torn jeans, and put on his new "store-bought's." Then he headed for the nearest saloon. His favorite drinks were whiskey and beer. On his drunken spree, the cowboy often terrorized the ordinary town citizens. Forget Hollywood fistfights—knives and manstoppers (guns) were the favorites. More often than not, the cowboy headed back to camp with an empty wallet and a sore head!

Hitting the saloon

Whether it was a tent, a Mexican *cantina*, or a false-fronted saloon, the bar was a place where men could relax, have a drink and a meal, play cards, or listen to music. Lonesome cowboys could pay a dollar to dance with a girl. Many saloons became famous, such as The Bucket of Blood Saloon, The Jersey Lily, and The Occidental.

In the bar

The bar took up most of the space, and it was well stocked with bottled wines, whiskey, and other spirits. There was home-brewed beer, as well as imported ale from England and stout from Ireland. The saloon sold home-baked food and luxuries such as pickled eggs or cheese.

▲ Cowboys loved to gamble. One rancher bet his ranch, livestock, and even his family on the turn of a card—he lost.

▲ *In Without Knocking*, by Charles Russell

Horsin' around

Cowboys were noted for bad behavior when they hit town. After months of hard work, they let off steam. The sheriff would lock up a drunken cowboy causing trouble and not let him out till he was sober.

With little money, cowboys would go to the cheaper saloons, while the cattlemen and stock buyers frequented fancy hotel bars. Hispanic and black cowboys were often forced to drink in separate saloons. Cow towns attracted all kinds: thieves, gamblers, gunmen, and outlaws. The Kansas cow town of Abilene employed respected lawmen like Wild Bill Hickok and Bat Masterson to keep the peace.

▼ The cow town was the place where the trail met the railroad. Towns like Wichita, Ellsworth, and Abilene flourished because of the cattle business. Stock buyers came from the East to buy whole herds to load on trains for New York and Chicago.

◄ To increase profits, bar owners would employ female singers. They'd be accompanied by a pianist, violinist, or banjo player. Some would put on a whole night of theatrical acts with jugglers and knife throwers.

WESTWARD HO!

Between 1836 and 1890, nearly 750,000 people crossed the western frontier. They came from all over the world, lured by the promise of land and a better future. The Mormons headed west to escape persecution and find their own Promised Land. They discovered it and settled in the Great Salt Lake region in Utah. And when gold was discovered in California in 1848, it sparked a rush of fortune-seekers.

Westward trails

With no highways to get from place to place, Native Americans and Spanish adventurers had to find their own way. Later, explorers and traders followed the same routes. Settlers' wagons widened them into dusty trails that formed a vast network across the prairies, deserts, and mountains of the West.

The trip from Independence to Oregon City covered 2,200 miles and took six months. Pioneers said: "The weak died on the way and courage never left."

There wasn't room on the wagon for everyone, and many made the long journey on foot. Wagons often broke down, and heavy furniture was discarded along the way to lighten the load.

Heading into unknown land had its dangers. Deaths by drowning, cholera, smallpox, and accidental shootings were all common. Many babies and young children didn't finish the trip. Livestock died of exhaustion or from eating poisonous plants. Hostile Native Americans would often steal cattle, oxen, and horses.

Stocking a Conestoga wagon didn't come cheap. Enough farming tools, furniture, food and clothing for a family of up to 16 could cost an incredible $1,500—almost five years' wages!

Staking a claim

At their journey's end, pioneers claimed their land by putting up a marker. The Homestead Act of 1862 allowed a settler 160 acres of land for just $10, so long as he stayed and improved the land for at least five years.

A soddy

It took 43,000 sq. ft. of sod to cut enough bricks to build a sod house or "soddy." The owners were nicknamed sodbusters.

Doors and windows

Doors were made from packing crates. Greased paper kept out the wind until the settlers could afford glass windows.

Making a home

Early pioneers built their homes with whatever nature provided. Log cabins were built in the forests of the Northwest, but on the plains there were few trees, so cavelike homes were dug into the sides of hills. These tended to collapse, so the "soddy" took their place. Once settlers could afford it, they built a more permanent structure.

Soddy life

Nature played havoc with sodbusters. Droughts were common; there were destructive twisters and dust storms. Plagues of locusts ate all the crops. During a summer storm, bolts of lightning might set the prairies on fire. In winter, blizzards froze the earth and the people.

Keeping warm

On the plains there were no logs to burn for cooking and heating. Sunflowers and greasewood might be used, but more often buffalo or cow "chips" (dung) were gathered. They made the house smelly, but at least everyone was warm!

It was hard work surviving as a pioneer family. Young children had to milk the cows, feed the chickens, and tend the horses. The lucky ones attended school, with older and younger children in one class. But they still had to do their chores. Illness and disease struck many families. Cholera and smallpox were killers. The nearest doctor might live many miles away, so the pioneers treated themselves with homemade remedies.

▲ Though work was shared by all, women did the cooking, cleaning, and washing as well as helping with the plowing and vegetables.

Water for life

Homesteaders couldn't survive without water. Some relied on a nearby river or creek, or collected rainwater in barrels. Others dug wells or used windmills to pump water out of the ground.

31

Lighter side of life

A visit to the general store was a family outing. The nearest shop could be up to 100 miles away, in the middle of nowhere, or in a town. Visiting the store was a chance to meet people as well as stock up on provisions.

The store

A typical general store stocked everything you could think of: dry goods, groceries, bolts of cloth, shoes, clothes, canned food, candy, lanterns, weapons, and farming tools. The shopkeeper provided chairs and a fire to make his customers feel welcome. People spent hours here catching up on news and gossip.

▼ A mother buys a bolt of cloth. She is going to make her daughter a new dress to wear at the Independence Day celebrations.

▼ A father thinks about buying a new Winchester carbine and shows it to his son. His old one has broken, and he needs the rifle for hunting and protection.

The wish book

Mail-order catalogs stocked everything from everyday items to luxuries. There was even a catalog for the lonesome man to order a bride from!

The quilting bee

Neighboring homesteads were far apart. Women took a break from the chores and gathered at one another's homes to swap gossip and make quilts. These "bees" lasted days: it could be a long time before they got together again.

All in a game

There were many ways that teenage boys could show off their strength and skills at the county fair. Pig-wrestling was dirty and fun. Other contests were frog-jumping competitions, foot races, games of catch, and even

Settlers liked to spend their limited spare time enjoying themselves. Every town in the United States held a parade to celebrate the Fourth of July. A wedding or a house- or barn-raising was a big event. And there were dances, horse races, boxing matches, and county fairs. There was plenty of food and drink, and a chance for people to meet old friends and make new ones.

Mine

In search of the rich veins of gold, miners used pickaxes and dynamite to dig cave-like mines in the mountainside. The rubble was then shoveled into the sluice.

Sluice

As the rubble from the mine passed down the long trough, water washed away the lighter debris to leave behind the heavier gold buried inside the rock.

Cash office

Inside the cash or assay office, gold dust and nuggets were weighed and traded for ready cash.

Laundry

Many Chinese were discriminated against in the gold fields. They found a way to make money out of the Gold Rush by opening camp laundries.

Fortunes

A typical miner working his own diggings could make lots of money. One ounce of gold was worth $16. Working seven days a week, a miner could find enough gold to earn himself almost $2,000.

Gold Rush!

"Gold! Gold on the American River!" With these words, Sam Brannan started the 1849 rush of fortune seekers to California. Some came overland along the Oregon Trail; others sailed to San Francisco. Known as the forty-niners, the prospectors included more than 17,000 Chinese immigrants. Mining camps, or diggings, sprang up with names like Sixbit Gulch, Whiskey Flat, and Hangtown.

Gold wasn't found only in California. The Black Hills of Dakota were sacred land to the tribes that lived there, and land that the government had promised them they could keep. But when the Seventh Cavalry explored the region, they found gold. News spread and thousands of gold seekers headed for the hills.

Community

At the diggings, miners of the same nationality soon found themselves living close together. They were very protective of their mines and looked after each other.

Muleback shack shop

Miners didn't have time to waste cooking luxuries like bread. So they were willing to part with a dollar a loaf when the baker came by with freshly baked bread. Women soon found they could make money by charging for meals. Some went on to be successful hotel owners.

▲ As fast as they sprang up, the mining towns also disappeared. Once every last bit of gold had been mined, there was nothing to keep people there. They packed their bags and headed for the next diggings, leaving a "ghost town" behind them.

Panning

There were easy ways to get gold out of the creek. One man would put rubble from the riverbed into a "rocker" as another man moved it back and forth in the flow of water. The gold was caught in a sieve below. Panning was a cheap and easy method. A handful of gravel or sand was put into a pan, then swirled around underwater to wash away the lighter sand, leaving the heavy gold behind.

KEY TO MAIN SITES OF TOMBSTONE

1. St. Paul's Episcopal church (under construction)
2. Mexican quarter
3. Hop Town—the Chinese quarter
4. New Cochise County courthouse (under construction)
5. C. S. Fly's photographic studio
6. Newspaper office: *Tombstone Epitaph*
7. City hall (under construction)
8. Original courthouse
9. Newspaper office: *Tombstone Nugget*
10. Theater: Schieffelin Hall
11. Post office
12. Jack Crabtree's Lexington livery stable
13. Catholic church (under construction)
14. Women's boardinghouses
15. Wells Fargo office
16. Ice cream parlor
17. O.K. Corral
18. U.S. customs office
19. Occidental Saloon
20. Watt & Tarbell's funeral parlor
21. The Crystal Palace Saloon (U.S. Deputy Marshal's office above)
22. The Oriental Saloon
23. City bakery
24. The Birdcage Theater
25. Western Union telegraph office
26. Courtroom
27. First public school (temporary)
28. Wing Woo Lung laundry
29. Miners' cabins
30. Fire station

Why "Tombstone?"

When Ed Schieffelin's party began prospecting in Arizona, someone said they were likely to find only tombstones. Instead, they struck silver, but used the name for the new settlement!

Frontier town

Not all towns in the West depended on the cattle trade for their existence. The discovery of rich mineral deposits could herald the birth of a frontier town. Tombstone, Arizona, began this way when silver was discovered there by prospector Ed Schieffelin in 1877.

Town folk

There were many people in town who depended on the success of Tombstone's mines for their livelihood. People of different cultures populated the town, so businesses had to cater to everyone's needs. There were newspapers, saloons, hotels, schools, and churches.

JOBS IN TOMBSTONE
1 Newspaper editor
2 Undertaker
3 Blacksmith
4 Traveling preacher
5 Actress
6 Schoolteacher
7 Mayor

Allen Street

Allen Street was one of Tombstone's main roads. It was lined with shops, hotels, banks, and saloons.

The street was nearly 80 feet wide. It had raised wooden sidewalks outside the stores and no street lights.

Tombstone is the site of the most famous gunfight in the West. Yet the gunfight at the O.K. Corral lasted only 30 seconds. After a long feud, Wyatt Earp, his brothers Morgan and Virgil, and Doc Holliday fought Ike and Billy Clanton, and Tom and Frank McLaury. The McLaurys and Billy Clanton were killed; Morgan and Virgil Earp and Doc Holliday were wounded.

A hard life

Many became soldiers to escape the law, poverty, or to start a new life. Army life was hard and many deserted. Poor supplies meant most food was maggot-infested. The soldiers lacked equipment and clothing. Only the officers lived in comfort. There was even a billiards room for them. The only entertainment for the ordinary soldiers was drinking in the bar.

▼ Hours of drill practice, either on foot or on horseback, took place on the parade-ground.

graveyard

cavalry stables

hospital

sutler's house

sutler's shop

bakery

officers' stables

camp store

storehouse

post office

barracks

laundries

icehouse

officers' quarters

parade-ground

commanding officer's quarters

barracks

icehouse

band room

guardhouse

The Laramie River protected the fort from attack.

Thanks to the hills behind it and its clear view across the plain, the fort was in little danger of surprise attack.

wood yard

hay yard

corral

mill yard

smithy

horse shed

Brown's hotel

Dakota camp

In early days Laramie was an important post on the northern plains, and a stop-off point for immigrants on the Oregon Trail. In 1849, it was bought by the government and became a fort.

Peacemaking powwows were held at Fort Laramie. The government made several treaties there with the Dakota and Arapaho, but none lasted very long.

FORT LIFE

As the United States expanded westward, the army was called in to protect the pioneers against Native Americans who were defending their homelands. Forts made important bases where the army could house its peacekeeping troops. They were well defended and rarely attacked. As the frontier grew, more and more forts were built, especially during the Indian wars. Many smaller defenses—called posts, garrisons, or camps—were built too, at strategic sites along the trails, such as river crossings or junctions.

Fort Davis, Texas
This campaign fort once housed black soldiers of the Ninth and Tenth Cavalry and the Twenty-fourth and Twenty-fifth Infantry. Abandoned in 1891, it is today a national monument.

Men at arms

 The protection of the United States in the early days was entrusted to a small army of professional soldiers and volunteer citizens. These men were not well trained or armed. Many were immigrants who were unable to speak English.

The army was responsible for survey parties, pioneers, the crews building the railroad, and defense of the territories. Even during the Civil War, when men went to fight for the North or South, the army still looked after the frontier.

◄ Corporal, U.S. Dragoons (1840s)

Mounted soldiers, such as the First Dragoons, protected the wagon trains from Indian attacks as they trundled along the Santa Fe Trail. They were issued with a single shot M1836 Hall Carbine .64 caliber and a wickedly sharp saber.

Buffalo soldiers

This painting by Frederic Remington is called *Buffalo Soldiers*. This nickname was given by the Native Americans to black soldiers, as their hair reminded them of buffalo hair: short and curly. There were four all-black units—two cavalry and two infantry.

► Private, Union Infantry (1861–1865)

The soldiers of the Union were fighting for a united country. Their blue uniform was standard issue, based on the early military design that got them the nickname of "blue bellies." When the Civil War came to an end, many soldiers were posted to the forts and garrisons in the West to keep the frontier open and fight in the Indian wars.

▶ Private, Infantry (1890s)

The soldier's uniform and weapons changed little over the years. The Springfield rifle was adapted from the Civil War muzzle-loader so it could take the same ammunition as the soldier's pistol. By the end of 1890 the soldier's job in the West was done. The Native Americans were defeated and the West settled.

The army was responsible for building roads and exploring new routes into the West. The Transportation Corps carried supplies and once even experimented with camels to carry loads in the desert! When Yellowstone National Park was established in 1872, the army was drafted in to look after that, too.

Call to arms!

The conflict between the Union North and Confederate South began in 1861 when Confederates attacked Union troops at Fort Sumter. Every able-bodied man was called to fight for his beliefs.

◀ Junior Officer, Confederate Cavalry (1862)

Often known as "Johnny Reb," the Confederate soldier fought for southern independence in the Civil War. The Confederates believed that they should be allowed to keep black slaves and that southern states should be free of northern government. Their "Rebel yell" was a bloodcurdling battle cry that frightened many soldiers of the Union.

Cap badges

Each regiment had its own distinctive badge, worn on the cap. The designs have hardly changed to this day.

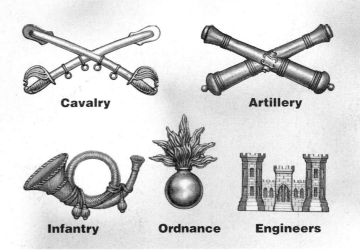

Cavalry

Artillery

Infantry

Ordnance

Engineers

Into battle

The army was famous for its campaigns against the Native Americans. Between 1865 and 1890 the conflict between the two sides brought many deaths. The army had more advanced weapons, but the American Indian tribes knew the lay of the land and were more mobile. The Battle of the Little Big Horn in 1876 was the most spectacular victory for the Native Americans, but it also proved to be their last.

"General" Custer
George Armstrong Custer was an eager soldier. He wanted to be a general, but reached only the permanent rank of lieutenant-colonel. He led the Seventh Cavalry in many victorious campaigns against the northern tribes until his death at the Battle of the Little Big Horn.

Sitting Bull
Tatonka-I-Yaktanka (Sitting Bull) was the medicine man of the Hunkpapa tribe of the Teton Dakota. He was also a politician who influenced the Cheyenne and Arapaho. He united the Dakota subtribes and became a feared and respected war chief.

Battle of the Little Big Horn
On June 22, 1876, against orders, Custer led the Seventh Cavalry in an attack on an Indian village at the Little Big Horn River, Montana. Led by great war chiefs such as Gall, Crazy Horse, and Sitting Bull, the Cheyenne and Dakota warriors killed Custer and all his men.

▲ *Custer's Last Stand*, by Edgar S. Paxson

In the battles after 1876 the army made a determined effort to beat the tribes into submission. With the defeat of Chief Joseph of the Nez Percé in 1877, white victory seemed certain. By the late 1880s only the Apaches were still fighting, led by such leaders as Cochise and Geronimo.

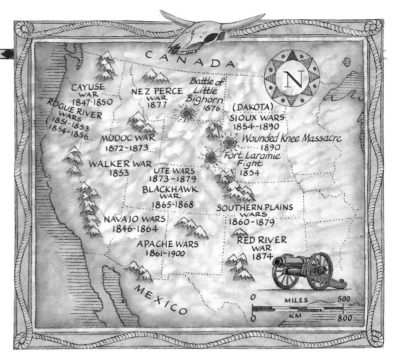

"The Great Father sends us presents and wants us to sell him the road, but the White Chief comes with soldiers to steal it before the Indian says yes or no. I will talk with you no more. I will go now and I will fight you!"

RED CLOUD

Indian wars

As white settlement increased, the government broke its promise to the Native Americans that it would claim only enough tribal land to allow the wagon trains to cross. Indian land was claimed for homesteads, railroads, and mines. Some tribes retaliated and attacked settlers, stagecoaches, and miners. The army was called in, and regional battles flared.

Massacre at Wounded Knee

On December 29, 1890, a unit of the Seventh Cavalry rounded up more than 300 Dakota at Wounded Knee Creek, South Dakota. As the soldiers were disarming the men, a shot was fired and the soldiers fired back. Within minutes the army had slaughtered the Dakota and ended the Native American opposition to the white Americans.

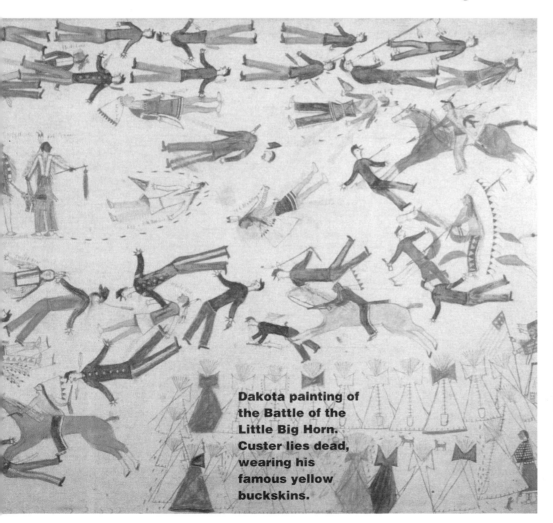

Dakota painting of the Battle of the Little Big Horn. Custer lies dead, wearing his famous yellow buckskins.

DEADLY DAYS

Outlaws were a threat to the frontier way of life. Some people stole rather than worked for a living. There were stagecoach robbers, rustlers, land barons who stole other people's claims, gamblers, and train robbers, to name a few.

Stagecoaches

Before the railroad was built, the stage was the main form of transportation for passengers and mail. There were many types of stagecoach, but none more famous than the Wells Fargo *Concorde*.

The loot

Money was carried on passenger stagecoaches. The strongbox held company payrolls in coins or gold, and this was the robbers' main target. Of course, they robbed the passengers too!

The gang

Outlaws operated alone or in gangs. The Hole in the Wall Gang—if records are to be believed—had over a hundred members from different gangs, including the Wild Bunch led by Butch Cassidy.

The one thing that an outlaw's life depended on was his weapon. Early revolvers, using paper cartridges with lead bullets, were classed as cap and ball pistols. These were later replaced with brass-jacketed bullets in different calibers. The revolver was used for fighting at close quarters. The rifle or carbine was useful for long-distance shooting. The threat of a shotgun was enough to scare anyone, and many outlaws sawed down the barrel to make the weapon easier to carry.

WEAPONS OF THE WEST
1 Loomis IXL No. 15 shotgun
2 Winchester M1866 carbine
   .44 caliber
3 Sharps M1863 carbine
   .52 caliber
4 Le Mat M1856
   .40 caliber
5 Walker Colt M1874
   .44 caliber
6 Colt New Model Army
   "Peacemaker" M1873
   .45 caliber
7 Smith & Wesson
   Model Army
   "Russian" No. 3
   revolver
   .44 caliber

WANTED APACHE KID

1867–c.1910

Once a cavalry scout, the Apache Kid killed a man, escaped, and went on to become a ruthless killer and robber who menaced New Mexico and Arizona.

WANTED BELLE STARR

1848–1889

Belle Starr was the leader of a gang of horse and cattle rustlers. She and her Cherokee husband, Sam, had a $1,000 reward on their heads.

WANTED WES HARDIN

1853–1895

Hardin was one of the most feared gunmen in Texas. After killing a black slave, he ambushed and killed the three Union soldiers sent to arrest him.

WANTED CATTLE ANNIE

1876–unknown

Cattle Annie once rode with the Doolin Gang. She and her partner, Little Britches, were famous cattle rustlers, known as "Oklahoma's girl bandits."

Billy the Kid (c.1859–1881)

He was only 22 years old when he died, but William H. Bonney, or Billy the Kid, left his mark. He killed his first man when he was 12 years old and was involved in a ranch war known as the Lincoln County War. After "the Kid" killed two deputies in New Mexico, Sheriff Pat Garrett hunted him down and shot him.

Outlaws and gunslingers

The best-known outlaws were the man-killers. Bloody Bill Anderson, Rufus Buck, Joaquin Murrieta, and John Brown were all cold-blooded murderers. After fighting in the Civil War, some, such as Frank and Jesse James, couldn't fit back in to normal civilian life. They took to robbery with a large gang of other ex-soldiers. Lone bandit Black Bart eluded the law for eight years robbing Wells Fargo stages. He had come to California to seek his fortune, and tried his hand at panning for gold before taking up his life of crime.

James Butler Hickok, or Wild Bill Hickok, was made into a living legend by newspapers and magazines. He was an army scout, Indian fighter, Pony Express employee, and lawman in several towns. He wore twin Colt Navy .36s in cross-draw fashion and was a deadly shot.

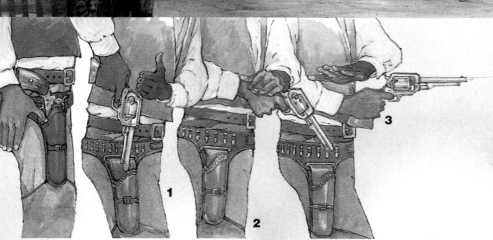

Fast on the draw

"Fanning" a revolver is the fastest way to fire more than one bullet. One hand grips the butt of the pistol, with the index finger holding back the trigger (1); the palm of the other hand hauls back (or "fans") the hammer (2). As the pistol comes up level, the hammer is fully cocked and springs forward at the same time (3).

Gunslingers

A gunslinger would use his pistol first and ask questions later. To be called a gunslinger meant that you were on the right side of the law, as well as a good man with a gun. Other names for these men were "gunsman," "gunny," and "gun shark." Whether he wore one pistol or two, the gunslinger always displayed his weapons to show he meant business.

Law and order

 Coping with criminals on the frontier was a problem. The area was too vast for the official police force. In some places ordinary men became vigilantes and fought the outlaws themselves. The Cattle Ranchers' Association hired range detectives to catch rustlers. Gunslingers were hired to guard banks, railroads, and mines. The most famous peace officer was the marshal. Towns hired marshals and deputies to enforce their laws.

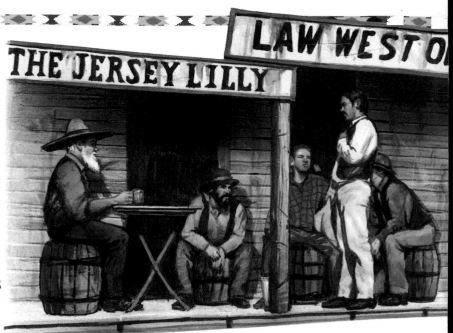

Law West of the Pecos

Roy Bean was nearly 60 when he came to the little town of Langtry, Texas. Self-taught in law, he set up a courtroom in his saloon, where he was judge for almost 20 years. He was in love with the English actress Lillie Langtry and named his saloon The Jersey Lily after her. The saloon sign was misspelled by a drunken cowboy, who painted it to work off one of Judge Bean's eccentric fines.

Badge of office

Law officers wore badges to show what job they held. There were as many designs as there were different jobs. A U.S. marshal was responsible for the whole state. The town marshal and deputies looked after the town for the government. The protection of local people, homes, and businesses was down to the sheriff and his deputies. The famed Texas Rangers were formed by Stephen F. Austin in 1823 to help enforce the law, and they still operate today.

Pinkerton

Civil War veteran Allen Pinkerton ran a detective agency that made a business out of capturing wanted men. The agency fought against the James Gang and the Wild Bunch. It was the first to keep files with details of solved and unsolved crimes and photographs of criminals, like the files used by the FBI today.

When criminals were caught they had to be punished, just like today. For lesser crimes, such as being drunk and disorderly, or carrying a weapon in public, there was just a fine. More serious crimes were punishable by death. Not all towns had jails; one prisoner was kept overnight under a tarpaulin staked to the ground! Some states issued an "invite to a necktie party," where the public could witness a hanging.

Own justice

Luke Short formed the Dodge City Peace Commission after being kicked out of town by the mayor because of the goings-on in his saloon. The commission, which included fellow-gunmen Bill Tilghman, Bat Masterson, Wyatt Earp, and Doc Holliday, among others, escorted Short back into town. With such strong backing, Short was allowed to run his saloon just as he pleased!

STEEL TRACKS

 Railroads were built to provide a speedy transportation system that spanned the continent. Their paths were often through Native American land, despite previous government promises, so troops had to guard the railroaders. Work started on the first transcontinental railroad in 1863. Ex-soldiers and Irishmen headed west from Omaha, building the Union Pacific line. Chinese railroaders headed east from San Francisco with the Central Pacific. On May 10, 1869, the two lines met at Promontory Point, Utah.

Railroad routes

Railroads were a fast way of transporting goods, mail, and people across deserts, prairies, and mountains. Cattle drives would end where their trail met the tracks. The map shows the railroad lines built in the 1860s and the towns that they connected.

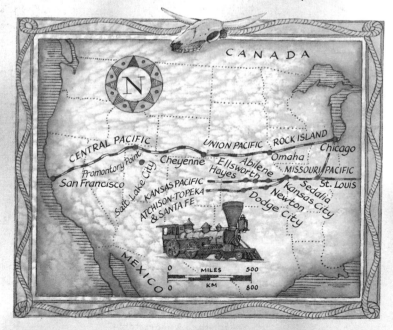

Explosion

Where tracks had to be laid through a mountain, specialist workers called graders blasted tunnels with dynamite. It was a dangerous job, and there were many accidents with the powerful explosives. Pickaxes and shovels were used too, and mule-drawn carts took away the rocks and rubble.

Communication

Railroad routes often followed the network of telegraph lines, so messages could be sent in seconds to company headquarters.

Camp

The railroad workers lived in makeshift towns, known as "hell on wheels." Most of the men slept in tents, which could be easily packed up.

Building skills

Obstacles such as valleys and rivers were no match for the engineers. They built trestle bridges of iron and wood, and suspension bridges spanning over 900 feet.

Supplies

Everything from food, water, rolling stock, and machinery to the rails themselves had to be taken to the site either by track already laid or by horse-drawn wagons.

As hard as they tried, the Native Americans couldn't stop the white man's "iron road."

The iron horse

▲ Cheap train tickets to the West.

The Native Americans called the train the iron horse. It was the classic American 4-4-0 steam locomotive that became the workhorse of the railroad. Passenger trains reached nearly 20 miles per hour, though heavily laden freight trains managed only half that speed.

A typical engine was over 50 feet long and powerful enough to haul the 40 tons of train. Behind the engine, the tender carried wood for the fire and over 2,000 gallons of water for the boiler that produced the steam to power the engine.

Pullman coach

tender

cab

Tickets and times

The fare from Kansas City to Denver cost $65 (six weeks' wages for a cowboy). Timetables showed the different routes, local times, and journeys. In 1863, the Railroad Association divided the country into the four time zones used today.

Trains replaced stages as the main way of carrying payrolls across the country. And, like stagecoaches, they got robbed. The first American train robbery took place in 1866 when the Reno Gang held up the Ohio and Mississippi Railroad and got away with $10,000.

▼ The engineer sounded a large steam whistle to warn of the train's approach.

safety valve

whistle

steam dome

bell

boiler

cylinder

spark-arrester

funnel

head-light

driving wheels

bogie wheels

cowcatcher

All aboard!

There was tough competition between the railroad companies. To attract customers, they advertised on colorful posters. They promised the fastest journey, most comfortable berths, or even that their crews were supplied with ammunition in case of attack!

In the driving seat

The engineer and the fireman stayed in the cab feeding the hungry fire in the engine with large wooden logs. The cab was built of varnished walnut and the engineer's seat of

Cowcatcher

A large metal triangle was fitted at the front of the train. The "cowcatcher" not only pushed stray cattle off the tracks; it also cleared any snowdrifts or loose rocks out of the way.

Spark-arrester

A wire mesh over the funnel stopped any stray sparks from escaping and setting the dry plains alight.

53

The end of the West

In 1890, the Bureau of the Census claimed that no frontiers remained in the United States. The days of the Wild West were over. No single factor decided it: the railroad now bridged East and West; the prairies and plains were settled; the Native Americans had been forced onto reservations. Yet the West was still growing. New rail routes were being built; Arizona and Utah were yet to join the Union; and immigrants still arrived in San Francisco in the thousands. This time the lure was not gold or land, but oil.

KEY

1 Makah 1855	44 Pueblo Indians 1858	83 Cherokee 1828
2 Ozette 1893	45 Zuni 1877	84 Peoria 1867
3 Quileute 1889	46 Mescalero Apache	84 Modoc 1874
4 Hoh River 1893	1873	84 Ottawa 1867
5 Quinalelt 1855	47 Hopi 1882	84 Shawnee 1831
6 Shoalwater 1865	48 Havasupai 1880	84 Seneca 1831
7 Chehalis 1864	49 Salt River 1879	84 Wyandot 1867
8 Umatilla 1855	50 Northern	85 Creek 1833
9 Grande Ronde 1857	Cheyenne 1884	86 Choctaw 1820
10 Warm Springs 1853	51 Colville 1872	87 Seminole 1833
11 Klamath 1864	52 Spokane 1881	88 Chickasaw 1837
12 Hoopa Valley 1864	53 Coeur d'Alene 1867	89 Kiowa &
13 Round Valley 1856	54 Jocko 1855	Comanche 1865
14 Pyramid Lake 1874	55 Blackfeet 1875	90 Winnebago 1865
15 Walker River 1874	56 Fort Belknap 1888	91 Omaha 1854
16 Tule River 1873	57 Fort Peck 1868	92 Red Lake 1863
17 Moapa River 1873	58 Crow 1868	93 White Earth 1867
18 Hualpai 1863	59 Crow Creek 1889	94 Vermilion Lake
19 Colorado River 1863	60 Lower Brule 1889	1881
20 Mission Indians 1875	61 Devil's Lake 1867	95 Mille Lac 1855
21 Gila Bend 1882	62 Turtle Mountain	96 La Pointe 1854
22 Yuma 1884	1882	97 Lac Courte
23 Gila River 1859	63 Fort Berthold 1870	Oreille 1854
24 Papago 1874	64 Standing Rock 1868	98 Ontonagon 1854
25 White Mountain 1871	65 Cheyenne River 1889	99 L'Anse 1854
26 Lummi 1855	66 Pine Ridge 1889	100 Lac du Flambeau
27 Swinomish 1855	67 Sioux 1882	1854
28 Tulalip 1855	68 Rosebud 1889	101 Menominee 1854
29 Puyallup 1854	69 Ponca 1881	102 Stockbridge
30 Muckleshoot 1857	70 Otoe & Missouri	1856
31 Squaxon Island 1854	1881	103 Isbella 1855
32 Skokomish 1855	71 Pawnee 1876	104 Tuscarora 1797
33 Port Madison 1855	72 Sac and Fox 1867	105 Tonawanda 1797
34 Yakima 1855	73 Iowa 1883	106 Cattaraugus 1797
35 Lapwal 1863	74 Pottawatomie 1867	107 Oil Spring 1797
36 Lemhl 1875	75 Wichita 1872	108 Allegany 1797
37 Uintah Valley 1861	76 Arapaho &	109 Onondaga 1788
38 Wind River 1861	Cheyenne 1869	110 Oneida 1788
39 Fort Hall 1868	77 Sac and Fox 1867	111 St. Regis 1796
40 Duck Valley 1877	78 Sac and Fox 1836	112 Eastern
41 Navaho 1868	79 Kickapoo 1832	Cherokee 1874
42 Ute 1863	80 Pottawatomie	113 Seminole 1894
43 Jicarilla Apache	1837	
1874	81 Kansas 1872	
	82 Osage 1870	

▲ The map shows the Native American reservations at the end of the century and the dates they were established. As their homelands were taken away, tribes were forced onto these reservations. Their traditional way of life was destroyed, and they could no longer support themselves.

Windmills

The settlers changed the face of the West. They brought water to the dry prairies, using windmill power to pump water from below ground. Desolate arid land was cultivated and became rich farmland.

Death of the range

The open-range style of raising cattle became a thing of the past as barbed-wire fenced in the land. Many ranchers turned to sheep farming: sheep were cheaper to keep, needed less labor and sold at higher profits.

Land rush

The last land rush, in 1899, was for Indian Territory in what is now Oklahoma. The Indians living there were finally driven onto reservations.

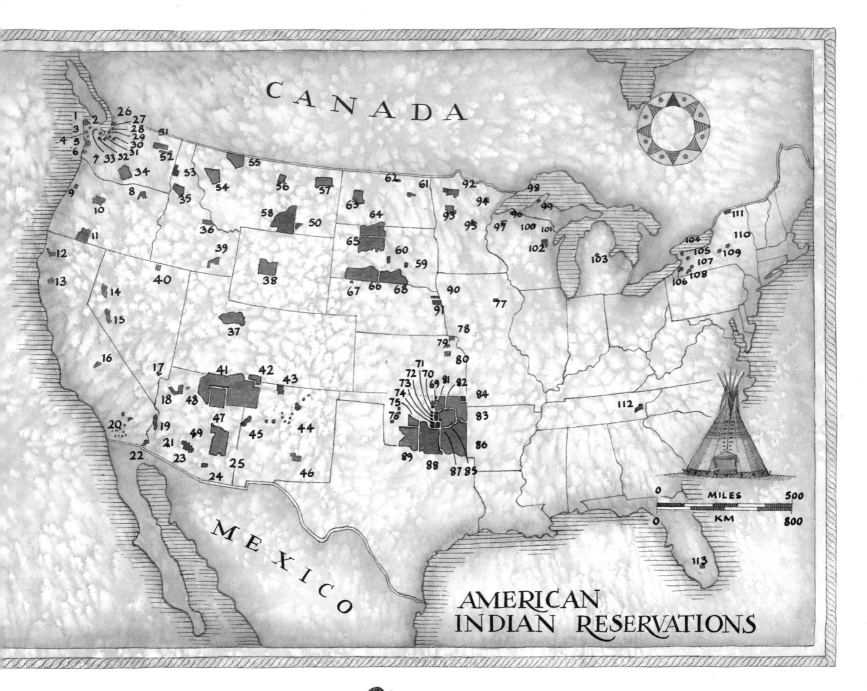

AMERICAN
INDIAN RESERVATIONS

Good-bye to the buffalo?

From 1872 to 1876, a staggering four million buffalo were killed. To preserve the dwindling herds, the government forbade buffalo hunting in Yellowstone Park, Wyoming, the country's first national park.

The outlaws

Lawlessness didn't stop with the closing of the frontiers. Such infamous outlaws as Butch Cassidy and the Sundance Kid continued to operate into the 1900s.

Gushing oil wells in Texas and California promised fortunes to be made. The first find was at Corsicana, Texas, in 1894. While drilling a well, workers struck oil instead. Fortune seekers poured into Texas just as the forty-niners had invaded California. Oil "fever" spread throughout the West and boomtowns sprang up. The West still promised wealth and a new life.

The entertaining West

Even as the Wild West was coming to an end, the legend was being born—there were rodeo events, books and magazines, and the first Wild West shows, such as Buffalo Bill's. All created an exciting image of the days of the frontier. Cinema and TV rediscovered the Wild West and presented daring—though not especially truthful—tales of heroes and villains.

1

2

3

4

Read all about it!

Authors and readers alike have found the West a rich source of exciting stories. Authors have used the West as a setting for romance (1), or to rewrite history with exaggerated tales of "cowboys and Indians" (2). Popular TV series created their own spin-offs for readers (3). Even at the time, cheap magazines and dime novels were churned out by the thousand. The soap operas of their day, these publications didn't paint an accurate picture of the West, but readers avidly followed the adventures of Pawnee Bill (4), Arizona Joe, and other heroes.

All the thrill of the show

Buffalo Bill Cody traveled the world with his Wild West Show in the 1880s. Whooping Native Americans, dashing cowboys, and mock stagecoach robberies thrilled huge audiences. Annie Oakley was one of the stars of the show. She was nicknamed "Little Miss Sure-Shot" by the Dakota chief Sitting Bull, who also toured with the show.

Rodeo riders

The rodeo is a dazzling contest of riding and roping skills. It started as an informal chance to show off. Today there are nearly 3,000 rodeo events around the world each year.

► Prairie Rose Henderson, 1900s: was she the first female broncobuster?

The West hits the small screen

Television series about the West peaked in the 1960s. "Bonanza" (above) was one of the most popular and ran for 14 years. Other well-loved TV shows included "Wagon Train," "The Lone Ranger," "Gunsmoke," "High Chaparral," and "Little House on the Prairie."

◄ **In 1881, Bill Pickett became the first cowboy to bulldog (wrestle) a steer.**

The first cowboy movies or "westerns" appeared in 1903. From the beginning, moviemakers chose to ignore the real West in favor of holdups and gunfights. These were far more exciting than the homesteaders' grinding toil! Frontier life was misrepresented in other ways too. According to Hollywood, there were no black or Native American cowboys. In the movie *Tomahawk*, black mountain man Jim Beckwourth was played by a white actor.

John Wayne

▼ **Not all Westerns are about cowboys.** *How the West Was Won* **(1962) tells the story of a pioneer family's struggle to settle the new land.**

Screen heroes

For many, the cowboy is typified by the heroic parts played by John Wayne, Clint Eastwood, and Kevin Costner. Early Hollywood movies portrayed the lone hero rather than the social network the cowboy depended on for his work—and sometimes his life. But where would Wyatt Earp be without his brothers, or Jesse James without his gang?

57

Characters of the West

Thomas Hart Benton
(1782–1858)
As a senator from the state of Missouri, he championed the cause of the United States's "Manifest Destiny"—the right to expand westward.

John Butterfield
(1801–1869)
Operated the Butterfield Overland Mail Service between Missouri and San Francisco from 1858 to 1861. He sold the firm to Wells Fargo and went on to develop a new venture—American Express.

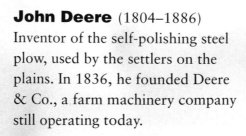

Martha Jane Canary (Calamity Jane)
(c. 1852–1903)
She was a good shot, often dressed as a man, and drove wagon teams for the Union Pacific Railroad. Stories abound about Jane, but she definitely loved Wild Bill Hickok and is buried next to him in Deadwood, Arizona.

Christopher (Kit) Carson
(1809–1868)
Famous as a fur trapper, explorer, scout, and Indian fighter, Carson spoke French, Spanish, and Indian languages.

Cochise (c. 1800–1874)
Renegade chief of the Chiricahua Apaches who led his warriors in raids on settlers and miners throughout Arizona and into Mexico.

William F. Cody (Buffalo Bill) (1846–1917)
The dime novelist Ned Buntline wrote of Buffalo Bill's exploits in 1869. Cody rode the Pony Express and was an army scout. In 1883 he began his famous Wild West Show.

Samuel Colt (1814–1862)
He designed a new, more reliable six-shooter by adapting the trigger and hammer action of the old five-shot revolver. His .45 "Peacemaker" was one of the most widely used guns in the West.

Crazy Horse (Tashunka Witco) (1842–1877)
One of the most aggressive Dakota chiefs, he fought at Rosebud and Little Big Horn.

George Crook (1828–1890)
Army general who led attacks against the Apache and Dakota in Mexico and Arizona. He tried to get better treatment for Geronimo and other Apaches after their surrender.

Isom Dart
(c. 1849–1900)
Born a slave, he fought with the Confederates and was a cattle rustler and broncobuster. He ended his days a rancher in Colorado.

John Deere (1804–1886)
Inventor of the self-polishing steel plow, used by the settlers on the plains. In 1836, he founded Deere & Co., a farm machinery company still operating today.

Wyatt Berry Stapp Earp
(1848–1929)
Lawman in Wichita, Dodge City, and Tombstone, who was best known for his involvement in the gunfight at the O.K. Corral. Earp later ran gambling halls and saloons.

Alice Fletcher (1838–1923)
A white woman who lived among Native American tribes in Nebraska. In 1883 she became an Indian agent and helped survey the land to be shared among the tribes. The Native Americans called her "Measuring Woman."

Captain John Charles Frémont (1813–1890)
Early explorer of the West, nicknamed "Great Pathfinder." Kit Carson was his guide. His wife's account of his journeys was a bestseller.

Pat F. Garrett (1850–1908)
Former buffalo hunter and cowboy, he was Sheriff of Lincoln County when he killed Billy the Kid. He later became a rancher and was shot dead in a feud.

Geronimo (Goyathly)
(1829–1909)
Chiricahua Apache who led his people against both Mexicans and Americans. He finally surrendered and lived on a Florida reservation from 1887.

Charles Goodnight
(1836–1929)
This fiery rancher was one of the great cattle barons. After success with Oliver Loving, he teamed up with John Adair in 1877. By 1888 he was worth $500,000.

Sam Houston (1793–1863)
He led the Texans at San Jacinto in the military drive to gain Texan independence from Mexico. In 1836 he was sworn in as the first president of the Republic of Texas.

Chief Joseph
(c. 1840–1904)
Unwilling to fight over land, Chief Joseph moved his tribe, the Nez Percés. The U.S. army pursued them, starting a three-month battle. The chief surrendered, and he and his tribe were put on a reservation.

Oliver Loving (1813–1867)
Before the Civil War he trailed herds to Colorado and Illinois. Loving did business with rancher Charles Goodnight from 1866.

Susan Shelby Magoffin
(1827–1855)
The first white woman to travel the Santa Fe Trail. She wrote a diary which was published in 1926.

James W. Marshall
(1810–1885)
A carpenter working in Sutter's Mill, California, Marshall was the first to discover gold there. This led to the Gold Rush of 1849.

William Barclay (Bat) Masterson (1853–1921)
Canadian lawman who found fame as a gambler. He was a Dodge City marshal.

Marie Gilbert (Lola) Montez (1818–1861)
Originally from Ireland, Lola was an actress of dazzling beauty who entertained the miners across the California gold region.

Annie Oakley (1860–1926)
She found fame in Buffalo Bill's Wild West Show as "Little Miss Sure-Shot." She could outshoot her husband, Frank Butler, a well-known exhibition marksman.

Isaac Parker (1838–1896)
An Arizona judge whose handling of outlaws soon got him the nickname of the "Hanging Judge." He even built a set of gallows that could hang more than one person at a time.

Red Cloud (1822–1909)
Dakota chief who successfully defended his land. He closed many settlers' routes, including the Bozeman Trail. He became leader of the reservation Indians, and after the signing of the Fort Laramie Treaty he forced the United States to keep its terms.

Sacajawea (c. 1787–1812)
A Shoshone Indian woman, she acted as a guide and interpreter for the explorers Lewis and Clark in their expedition of 1804–1806.

William Tecumseh Sherman (1820–1891)
A Union general famed for his Civil War exploits. After the Civil War, Sherman took control of building forts across the West. He was in charge of the entire U.S. army between 1869 and 1884 and led the soldiers in many of the Indian wars.

John B. Stetson (1830–1906)
Hatmaker from Philadelphia. His famous hat, the Stetson, was sometimes also called Boss of the Plains, a John B, or a JB.

William Matthew Tilghman (1854–1924)
Renowned as a buffalo hunter and crack shot, he served as Dodge City's first marshal. He moved to Oklahoma, where he was one of the "Three Guardsmen" (along with Chris Madsen and Heck Thomas) who hunted down the Doolin and Dalton gangs.

Sarah Winnemucca
(1844–1891)
Paiute who negotiated for better conditions for her tribe. In 1883 she wrote an autobiography, *Life Among the Paiutes*, telling of their plight.

Brigham Young (1801–1877)
Religious leader who led the Mormons from Nauvoo, Illinois, where they were being persecuted for their beliefs, to Utah to settle on the shores of the Great Salt Lake.

Glossary

assay office Place where miners weighed and priced their gold.

barracks Soldiers' sleeping quarters.

brand The mark burned into the hide of a cow or horse to show who owned it.

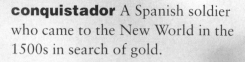

BRAND

bronco A wild horse, a mustang.

broncobuster Someone who tamed wild, "unbroken" horses for cowboys to ride.

buffalo Shaggy wild cattle, also known as bison.

buffalo chip Dried buffalo dung used as fuel on the plains.

caliber The diameter of a bullet.

cap and ball Early revolver, loaded at the front of the cylinder.

carbine A short light rifle.

cartridge A small case holding gunpowder or bullets.

cattle baron Someone who owned a vast cattle empire. Also known as a cattle king.

cattle drive A herd of cattle traveling across a trail to be sold.

chaps Tough leggings worn over a cowboy's trousers to protect the legs.

chuck wagon A mobile cook-house used on roundups and cattle drives. The chuck box at the back stored food, utensils, and medicine.

claim To have the legal right over the ownership of a mine, farm, or grazing land.

Conestoga wagon A boat-shaped load-carrying wagon used by the pioneers, usually pulled by oxen.

conquistador A Spanish soldier who came to the New World in the 1500s in search of gold.

corral Fenced enclosure for cattle or horses.

coup stick A long, lancelike stick with a curved end used by Native American warriors to touch their enemy but not kill.

cow town A town that sprang up on a cattle trail, also known as a trail town or cattle town.

cross draw Style of drawing a revolver in which the holster is worn on the hip with the butt of the revolver facing forward. The hand crosses in front of the body to draw the revolver.

dogie (1) An orphan calf. (2) Nickname for cattle.

fanning A method of shooting a revolver quickly by pulling back the hammer and pulling the trigger at the same time.

fort A military base.

frontier The farthest edge of land that is settled, beyond which the country is wild.

gallows A purpose-built structure to hang people.

greasewood A low, stiff shrub that grows wild in the West, sometimes used as firewood.

Great Father Name for the President of the United States used by Native Americans.

gunslinger A fighter especially skilled with a gun.

holster A pouch to hold a revolver.

land baron A man who seized land, sometimes not very honestly.

lariat A rope used for catching animals. Known around the West Coast as a lasso.

line rider A cowboy who rode to the farthest limit (the line) of a ranch, to stop cows from straying.

loot Stolen goods.

lynch To punish someone without a proper trial, usually by hanging.

LARIAT

marshal A town's law-enforcer.

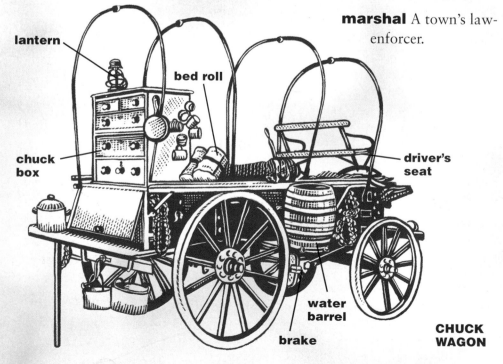

lantern

bed roll

chuck box

driver's seat

water barrel

brake

CHUCK WAGON

maverick A calf without a brand.

Mormon A member of the Church of Jesus Christ of Latter-Day Saints, established in 1830.

panning Washing gravel in a pan so only the gold or silver is left behind.

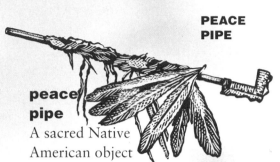

PEACE PIPE

peace pipe A sacred Native American object that invoked spiritual power when smoked. Also called a medicine pipe.

pemmican Native American preserved food made of meat, berries, and fat.

Pony Express A mail service between Missouri and California in 1860 and 1861. Riders carried mail along the 1,962-mile trail in less than ten days.

powwow A ceremonial gathering of Native Americans for war, for peace talks, to socialize, or to dance.

prairie Open grassland.

Pullman coach The locomotive passenger coach built by the Pullman Company.

ranch A cattle farm. It includes all the land, buildings, and animals owned by the rancher.

remuda A herd of spare horses for cowboys.

Rendezvous The meeting between trappers and Native Americans held every summer.

reservation Land put aside by the government for the use of one or more Native American tribes.

revolver A handgun, often known as a six-shooter or pistol.

rocker A box or cradle used by gold miners. Gravel and water were rocked back and forth to sift out the dirt, leaving the gold behind.

rodeo A contest of cowboy skills.

roundup The gathering together of cattle for branding by cowboys.

rustler A cattle or horse thief.

scout A guide or lookout.

settler Someone who makes a home in a place that is being populated for the first time. Also known as a pioneer.

skillet A metal frying pan.

slicker A waterproof coat.

soddy A dwelling made of sod built by settlers.

sougan A cowboy's closely woven or quilted blanket.

stagecoach A horse-drawn coach that carried passengers and mail.

steer A male cow that is raised for beef.

Stetson A broad-brimmed, high-crowned felt hat, named after the hatmaker John B. Stetson.

stickball An early Native American hockey-like game, on which lacrosse is based.

sutler A trader at an army post.

telegraph A means of sending Morse code messages electronically along a wire.

Texas tick A fever in Texas longhorn cattle that made them sick.

barrel

REVOLVER

hammer

chamber

trigger

butt

tomahawk A Native American war ax.

totem Native American name for an animal, such as an eagle, or a thing, such as a river, considered to be a spiritual ancestor.

trapper Someone who made a living catching beaver and other wild animals for their fur.

tribe A community of Native Americans who speak the same language and are bound together by ties of blood.

vaquero The name for a cowboy in the Southwest.

vigil A religious ceremony to mark a Native American child's passage into adulthood.

vigilante Someone who takes the law into their own hands to gain justice.

STETSON

war chief A Native American leader in time of war, usually younger and less experienced than the chief of a tribe.

Wells Fargo Stagecoach company founded in 1852.

Winchester A rifle made by the Winchester Repeating Arms Co., known as "the rifle that won the West."

wish book A mail-order catalog.

wrangler A man or boy who looked after the horses on a ranch or trail drive.

Index

Acknowledgments

The publishers would like to thank the following
illustrators for their contributions to this book:

Richard Berridge (Specs Art) 20–21, 22*b*, 23*b*, 24–25, 26–27;
Peter Dennis (Linda Rogers Associates) 4–5, 6, 7*l*, 28–29, 30–31, 32,
33, 34–35; **Terry Gabbey** (Associated Freelance Artists Ltd.) 10–11,
14–15, 16, 18–19, 50–51, 52–53, 56–57*b*; **Luigi Galante** (Virgil
Pomfret Agency) 36–37, 38–39; **Christian Hook** 44–45, 46*br*, 47,
48*tr*, 49; **John Lawrence** (Virgil Pomfret Agency) 58–59, 60–61;
Malcolm McGregor 7*br*, 8, 14*tr*, 15*tr*, 17*l/m*, 21*b*, 23*m*, 40–41, 45*br*,
48*bl*; **Tim Slade** 4–5*t*, 5*br*, 13, 25*tl*, 28*bl*, 43*t*, 50*bl*, 54–55*t*; **Peter
Thoms** 25*br*; **Shirley Tourret** (B. L. Kearley Ltd.) 9*tr/br*, 12, 13*r*,
16–17*t*, 17*r*, 21*t*, 22*tr*, 23*tl*, 25*tr*, 30*tl*, 37*m*,
42*t*, 43*br*, 46*l*, 47*b*, 54–55*b*

Engravings by **John Lawrence** (Virgil Pomfret Agency)
Decorative border by **Mark Peppé** (B. L. Kearley Ltd.)

The publishers would also like to thank the following for supplying
photographs for this book:

Amon Carter Museum: 15*tl* *Indian Girls Grinding Corn*
Adam R. Vroman; 27*tl* *In Without Knocking* Charles M. Russell;
Bridgeman Art Library: 56*tr*; **Buffalo Bill Historical Center**:
42*bl* *Custer's Last Stand* Edgar S. Paxson; **J. Allan Cash**: 8*t*;
Corbis/Bettman (U.K.): 25*bl*; 31*t*; 33*tl*; 40*bl* *Buffalo Soldiers* Frederic
Remington; 41*r*; 42*tr*; 56*r*; **Empire Interactive**: 57*br* Gettysburg;
Werner Forman (N. J. Saunders): 8*t*; **Ronald Grant Archive**: 57*tl*;
Kobal Collection: 57*r* & *bl*; **Montana Historical Society**: 27*br* *At the
Railhead*; **Peter Newark's Western Americana**: endpaper *Driving the
Golden Spike at Promontory, Utah, May 10, 1869*; 7*r Fall of the
Alamo* Robert Onderdonk; 9*tl The Cowboy* Frederic Remington; 33*tl*;
37*bl*; 48*br*; 52*t*; 53*r*; 56*l*, *bl/r*; **Laurence Parent**: 39*br*; **Southwest
Museum**: 42–3*b The Battle of the Little Big Horn* Kicking Bear; **State
Historical Society of North Dakota**: 33*tr Pendroy Quilting Party*;
Trip/Art Directors: 35*tr*;

and **Fort Laramie** for their kind assistance.